THE
DALMATIAN

by Charlotte Wilcox

Content Consultant
Julie Lux
Public Relations Officer
Dalmatian Club of America

C A P S T O N E   P R E S S
M A N K A T O ,   M I N N E S O T A

C A P S T O N E   P R E S S

818 North Willow Street • Mankato, MN 56001

http://www.capstone-press.com

Printed in the United States of America.

Library of Congress Cataloging-in-Publication Data
Wilcox, Charlotte.
    The dalmatian / by Charlotte Wilcox
    p. cm.--(Learning about dogs)
    Includes bibliographical references and index.
    Summary: Discusses the history, physical characteristics, care, and breeding of this dog known for its distinctive spots.
    ISBN 1-56065-541-0
    1. Dalmatian dog--Juvenile literature. [1. Dalmatian dog. 2. Dogs.]
    I. Title. II. Series: Wilcox, Charlotte. Learning about dogs.
SF429.D3W553 1998
636.72--dc21

                                          97-8316
                                            CIP
                                             AC

Photo credits
Reynolds Photography, cover
Brian Beck, 6
Cheryl A. Ertelt, 22
Mark Raycroft, 4, 14, 18, 26, 28, 38, 40-41
Cheryl R. Richter, 9, 34
Unicorn/Jean Higgins, 10; Tommy Dodson, 12;
    Roger Jennings, 17; Angel Vohra 20 ; Gary L. Johnson, 25;
    James L. Fly, 31; Eric R. Berndt, 32; Tom McCarthy 36

Table of Contents

Quick Facts about the Dalmatian...................... 4

Chapter 1 A Lot of Spots 7

Chapter 2 The History of the Dalmatian 13

Chapter 3 The Dalmatian Today 23

Chapter 4 The Dalmatian in Action 29

Chapter 5 Owning a Dalmatian...................... 35

Photo Diagram.. 40

Quick Facts about Dogs................................... 42

Words to Know 44

To Learn More 45

Useful Addresses 46

Internet Sites.. 47

Index 48

Quick Facts about the Dalmatian

Description

Height: Dalmatians stand 19 to 24 inches (48 to 61 centimeters) tall. Height is measured from the ground to the withers. The withers are the tops of the shoulders.

Weight: Dalmatians weigh 40 to 70 pounds (18 to 31.5 kilograms). Females are smaller than males.

Physical features: Most people recognize dalmatians by their spots. They have short, sleek coats. They have drop ears and long tails.

Color: Dalmatians are white with black or liver colored spots. Liver is a dark reddish brown.

Development

Place of origin: No one knows for sure where the dalmatian breed came from. Dalmatians may be named for Dalmatia, a region in Croatia. Or they may be named after a Serbian poet and dog breeder, Jurij Dalmatin.

History of breed: Dalmatians were used as coach dogs because they got along well with horses.

Numbers: More than 35,000 dalmatians are registered every year in the United States. Register means to record a dog's breeding records with an official club. About 1,500 dalmatians are registered each year in Canada.

Uses

Most dalmatians are pets. Some fire departments keep them for mascots. A mascot is something kept by a group for good luck. Dalmatians are used as watchdogs and for search and rescue. They are also great circus performers. A few are guide dogs for the blind.

Chapter 1
A Lot of Spots

It is easy to spot a dalmatian. People recognize dalmatians by their spots. The dalmatian's spots are like no other breed's.

Even people who know little about dogs know a dalmatian when they see one. This is partly because of a popular children's story. In 1956, Dodie Smith wrote a book called *The Hundred and One Dalmatians*. Walt Disney made a cartoon version five years later.

In the story, a woman wanted to use dalmatians for fur coats. There is no evidence that dalmatian fur was ever really used for clothing. People just like to look at these dogs' beautiful spotted coats.

No other breed of dog has spots like a dalmatian's.

But spots are only one reason dalmatians are well known. They are more than good looking. They are friendly and usually well behaved. They can run for hours without getting tired. They are one of the few breeds that can keep up with horses. In fact, dalmatians have a special relationship with horses.

Dalmatians and Horses

Many dogs do not get along well with horses. Some dogs are afraid of horses. Others try to chase or frighten horses. But dalmatians seem to understand and love horses.

Horses accept dalmatians. They do not accept any other dog breed. Even a dalmatian with no training will naturally follow a horse.

In horse-and-buggy days, dalmatians had an important job. They were special friends of the horses who pulled carriages. Dalmatians slept in the stables with the horses. They ran along with the horses as they pulled carriages.

Dalmatians can run for hours without getting tired.

Dalmatians protected the people riding in the coach. When people left the coach, they did not have to worry about their things. They knew the dalmatians would guard them.

This job earned dalmatians the name coach dog. No other breed has ever been used for that purpose. Today, few people drive horses and buggies. But many people still enjoy keeping dalmatians as pets.

Many people enjoy keeping dalmatians as pets.

Chapter 2
The History of the Dalmatian

No one knows for sure where dalmatians came from. A dog that looks like a dalmatian was found in an Egyptian drawing. The drawing is thousands of years old. It shows a spotted dog running behind a cart pulled by horses.

The Dalmatia Connection
Dalmatians might have been named after a place called Dalmatia. This is a narrow region on the coast of Croatia. Croatia is in eastern Europe. The people of Dalmatia may have raised spotted hunting dogs. But few spotted dogs live in Dalmatia today.

No one knows for sure where dalmatians came from.

Dalmatians may have been named after Jurij Dalmatin. He was a poet who lived in Serbia about 400 years ago. Serbia is in eastern Europe. In 1573, someone gave Dalmatin two dogs. The dogs came from Turkey.

Dalmatin bred the dogs. He started a breed that was called by his name. However, it is not certain that Dalmatin's dogs were like the dalmatians of today.

The Gypsy Dog

Some of the earliest people known to keep dalmatians were the Gypsies. This is an ethnic group that originated in India.

The Gypsies left India about 500 years ago. They wandered in Europe. Later, some Gypsies came to North America. But most of them stayed in Europe. For hundreds of years, they lived in groups and traveled in horse-drawn wagons.

No one knows if Gypsies had dalmatians from the beginning. They may have brought

No one is sure where dalmatians got their name.

15

their dogs with them from India. The dalmatian was sometimes called the harrier of Bengal. A harrier is a dog that chases hares or rabbits. Bengal is part of India.

The Gypsies may have adopted dalmatians from somewhere else during their travels. Either way, the Gypsies introduced the spotted dogs to Europeans.

The Coach Dog

Europeans realized that dalmatians have a special way with horses. By the 1700s, most wealthy Europeans had dalmatians. Some dalmatians were used with riding horses for hunting. Others were trained to run with carriages pulled by horses.

Many carriages were pulled by four horses. The two in front were called lead horses. The two behind were called wheel horses. Usually the dog ran between the wheels of the carriage. Some dalmatians could run in the middle of these horses, between the lead team and the wheel team.

The dalmatian was once called the harrier of Bengal.

Dalmatians are found as mascots for fire stations across North America and Canada.

Only the smartest dalmatians became coach dogs. If a dog fell out of step, it could be run over by a wheel or trampled by a horse.

The horses and dalmatians stayed together all the time. They became lifelong friends. When people traveled long distances, dalmatians guarded their carriage when it stopped for the night.

People came to North America from Europe in the 1700s. They brought their best horses and dogs with them. This included a few dalmatians. George Washington had a dalmatian. But the breed was not common in North America. This changed in the 1800s.

The Fire Dog

As more people settled in North America, towns sprang up everywhere. Most buildings were made of wood. Fire was a great danger. Every town needed a fire department. The fire station held a fire wagon and horses to pull it.

Before automobiles, fire wagons were the only way to get fire fighters and their supplies to a fire. The fastest horses were chosen to pull fire wagons. When the fire whistle blew, they had to be ready to run at a moment's notice.

Fire fighters in London, England, were the first to discover that dalmatians were perfect companions for them and their horses. The gentle, friendly dogs kept people and horses from being bored. They also kept rats and mice away. Soon fire stations all across

England and North America had dalmatians.

But dalmatians had an even more important job during the early days of fire fighting. They ran ahead of the speeding horses to clear the way. Dalmatians running down the road were like flashing lights and sirens today. Everyone moved out of the way in a hurry.

The combination of dalmatians, horses, and fire fighters made the local fire station a popular place. Children begged to visit the fire station when they came to town. They gave treats to the horses and dogs. They listened to the fire fighters tell of their adventures.

Dalmatians helped make fire stations popular places for children.

Chapter 3

The Dalmatian Today

Fire fighters no longer need horses to haul their supplies. But many still keep a dalmatian or two at the fire department. The dogs represent the proud history of fire fighting.

Features of a Dalmatian

Dalmatians are medium-sized dogs. They are 19 to 24 inches (48 to 61 centimeters) tall. Height is measured from the ground to the withers.

Dalmatians are muscular dogs. They have deep chests and strong bones. Dalmatians weigh 40 to 70 pounds (18 to 31.5 kilograms). Females are smaller than males.

Dalmatians have medium-sized ears that fold down close to the head. Their tails are long and come to a point at the tip. Their coats are short and glossy.

Dalmatians have ears that fold down close to the head.

Dalmatians have brown or blue eyes. Dogs with black spots usually have darker eyes than dogs with liver-colored spots. The areas around the eyes and nose are always the same color as the spots.

The Dalmatian's Spots

Most dalmatians are born with pure white coats. The spots appear gradually over the first few weeks of the dalmatian's life.

Dalmatian spots are round. They can be the size of a dime up to the size of a half-dollar. Some dalmatians get both black and liver spots. Some are born with a very large black or brown marking called a patch.

Dalmatians with patches or spots of two colors are not used for breeding. They might pass their coloring on to their puppies. Dog clubs consider this bad coloring, but these dogs are still good pets.

Most dalmatians are born without their spots.

Health Concerns

Dalmatians are strong and healthy. They have a lot of endurance. But their urinary system is different from other dogs. A urinary system is the way a body rids itself of liquid waste. A chemical called uric acid builds up in the urine of dalmatians. Other dog breeds do not have this problem.

Uric acid forms lumps called stones in the urinary tract. This is often painful. Large stones can lead to death. Dalmatians must drink plenty of water. They must urinate often. They must get a lot of exercise. These steps help keep uric acid from building up. A special diet can also help.

About one-third of all dalmatians are born deaf in one or both ears. Dalmatian puppies should be tested for deafness by a veterinarian when they are six weeks old. A veterinarian is a person trained and qualified to treat the sicknesses and injuries of animals.

Dalmatians that are deaf in only one ear make fine pets. But they should not be bred. They could pass the deafness on to their puppies. Dalmatians that are deaf in both ears are usually put to sleep.

About one-third of all dalmatians are born deaf in one or both ears.

Chapter 4

The Dalmatian in Action

Dalmatians still keep fire fighters company. They are favorites of children who visit fire stations. Dalmatians sometimes visit schools with fire fighters. They ride in the fire trucks during parades. Sometimes they do more important things.

Search and Rescue

Some fire departments train dalmatians to carry supplies into burning buildings. They also search for trapped people. They can smell a person even when the air is filled with smoke.

Fire departments train dalmatians to carry supplies into burning buildings.

Jack was a dalmatian hero. He lived with Engine Company 105 in Brooklyn, New York. One day, a child fell in front of a fire truck in Jack's station. The truck was about to speed out of the station to a fire. Jack saw the child and jumped to action. He rolled the child out of the truck's way. Jack received a Medal of Valor for his rescue.

Army Dogs

The U.S. Army used dalmatians to guard military camps during World War I (1914-1918), World War II (1939-1945), and the Vietnam War (1954-1975). Dalmatians are very protective. This makes them good watchdogs.

The British army used dalmatians to carry messages during World War II. An army officer would tie a message to the dog's collar. Then the officer would give the dog a command to travel to another camp.

Dalmatians were good at this job. But there was one problem. The dalmatians' white coats made them easy targets for enemy guns. The British colored the dogs brown so they could not be seen easily.

Dalmatians that work with fire fighters sometimes become heros.

Road Trials

The Dalmatian Club of America sponsors exciting events called road trials. These are competitions in which dalmatians use their greatest natural talent. They run with horses.

At a road trial, dalmatians run along with horseback riders or horses pulling carriages. Trials are 12.5 miles (20 kilometers) or 25 miles (40 kilometers). Dogs are judged on how well they perform and behave on the road. They also earn points for speed.

Everyday Fun

Dalmatians are one of the best breeds for bicyclers and runners. A dalmatian can run for long distances. Hikers and backpackers like dalmatians, too. Dalmatians are strong enough to carry small backpacks.

Dalmatians are one of the best breeds for runners.

Chapter 5

Owning a Dalmatian

Dalmatians are easy to get along with. They need a lot of exercise. Running is in their nature. For many centuries they were bred to run for hours at a time.

Keeping a Dalmatian

Dalmatians make excellent living companions for people. They do not do well outside in cold weather. Dalmatians need a lot of activity. They can become troublemakers if they do not get enough exercise. They need to be walked two to five miles (three to eight kilometers) every day.

Indoors, a dalmatian needs a special place all its own. Baskets, dog beds, and crates work well. If a dalmatian must stay home alone, a crate is the best choice.

Dalmatians make excellent living companions for people.

Dalmatians require a lot of care.

The Dalmatian's Diet

Dalmatians must eat a diet that does not produce uric acid. A good choice is dry dog food that does not contain liver, beef, or dairy products. The amount of food needed depends on the size and activity level of the dog. An average full-grown dalmatian may eat about one pound (about half a kilogram) of dry food a day.

Dalmatians need more water than other breeds. This helps keep uric acid from building up. Some owners add two to three cups (one-half to one liter) of water to the dry food. They do this to make sure their dog gets extra water.

Grooming

Dalmatians are naturally clean. They do not have a strong dog odor. But they do shed. They must be brushed every day. This helps keep their hair off furniture and clothing. A five-minute brushing will remove the loose hair. The brushing should be done outside.

Baths can bother a dalmatian's skin. Dalmatians should not have more than three or four baths per year.

The dog's anal sacs also need care. These are glands located on either side of a dog's rectum. The glands release a scent that dogs use to mark their territory. These glands can become blocked. If they are not opened up, they can become infected.

If a dog drags itself around on its rear end, the glands may need attention. Gently squeezing

It is important to buy a dalmatian puppy from a good breeder.

the glands can open them up. A veterinarian can show a dog owner how this is done.

Finding a Dalmatian

A dalmatian must be introduced to humans right away. If it is not, it may not make a good pet.

The movie *101 Dalmatians* caused an increase in demand for dalmatians. Some people

started breeding dalmatians just to sell
the puppies.

Some of these breeders did not consider the
importance of breeding for good qualities. Some
did not know about deafness. Others did not
introduce their puppies into their own family
when the dogs were small.

It is important to buy a puppy from a good
breeder. The Dalmatian Club of America or the
American Kennel Club can provide names of
good breeders.

Dalmatians can also be found at rescue
shelters. A rescue shelter is a home for dogs that
were abandoned.

Breeders sometimes have adults dogs for sale.
They may have been unsuccessful as show dogs.
Or they might be unable to have puppies. But
these dalmatians can still make excellent pets.

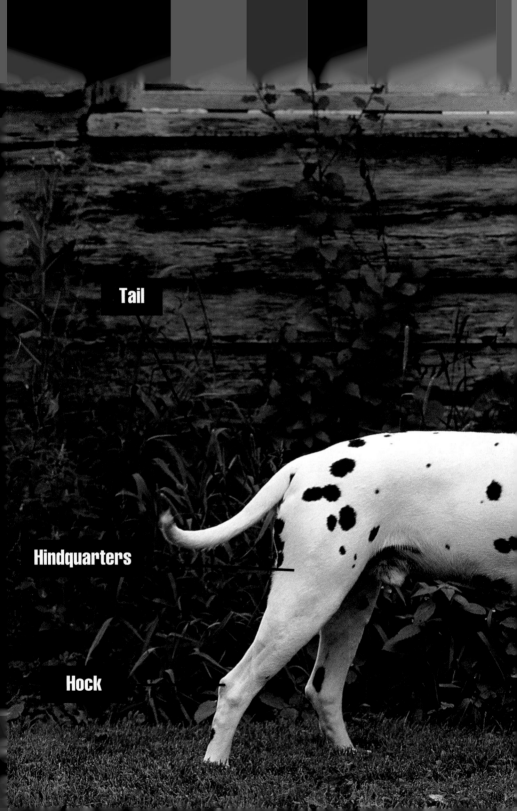

Tail

Hindquarters

Hock

Quick Facts about Dogs

Dog Terms

A male dog is called a dog. A female dog is known as a bitch. A young dog is a puppy until it is one year old. A newborn puppy is a whelp until it no longer depends on its mother's milk. A family of puppies born at one time is called a litter.

Life History

Origin: All dogs, wolves, coyotes, and dingoes descended from a single wolflike species. Dogs have been friends of humans since earliest times.

Types: There are many colors, shapes, and sizes of dogs. Full-grown dogs weigh from two pounds (one kilogram) to more than 200 pounds (90 kilograms). They are from six inches (15 centimeters) to three feet (90 centimeters) tall. They can have thick hair or almost no hair, long or short legs, and many types of ears, faces, and tails. There are about 350 different dog breeds in the world.

Reproductive life: Dogs mature at six to 18 months. Puppies are born two months after breeding. A female can have two litters per year. An average litter is three to six puppies, but litters of 15 or more are possible.

Development: Puppies are born blind and deaf. Their ears and eyes open at one to two weeks. They try to walk at about two weeks. At three weeks, their teeth begin to come in.

| Life span: | Dogs are fully grown at two years. If well cared for, they may live up to 15 years. |

The Dog's Super Senses

Smell:	Dogs have a sense of smell many times stronger than a human's. Dogs use their sensitive noses even more than their eyes and ears. They recognize people, animals, and objects just by smelling them. Sometimes they recognize them from long distances or for days afterward.
Hearing:	Dogs hear better than humans. Not only can dogs hear things from farther away, they can hear high-pitched sounds people cannot.
Sight:	Dogs are probably color-blind. Some scientists think dogs can see some colors. Others think dogs see everything in black and white. Dogs can see twice as wide around them as humans can because their eyes are on the sides of their heads.
Touch:	Dogs enjoy being petted more than almost any other animal. They can feel vibrations like an approaching train or an earthquake about to happen.
Taste:	Dogs do not taste much. This is partly because their sense of smell is so strong that it overpowers their taste. It is also because they swallow their food too quickly to taste it well.
Navigation:	Dogs can often find their way through crowded streets or across miles of wilderness without any guidance. This is a special dog ability that scientists do not fully understand.

Words to Know

anal sacs (AY-nuhl SAKS)—glands on either side of a dog's rectum, containing scent fluids

coach dog (KOHCH DAWG)—a dog that runs alongside or underneath a carriage pulled by horses

mascot (MASS-kot)—something kept by a group for good luck

register (REJ-uh-stur)—to record a dog's breeding records with an official club

uric acid (YUR-ik ASS-id)—a chemical produced in the urine of mammals

urinary system (YOOR-uh-nar-ee SISS-tuhm)—the way a body rids itself of liquid waste

veterinarian (vet-ur-uh-NER-ee-uhn)—a person trained and qualified to treat sicknesses and injuries of animals

wean (WEEN)—to stop depending on a mother's milk

withers (WITH-urs)—the top of an animal's shoulders

To Learn More

Smith, Dodie. *The Hundred and One Dalmatians*. New York: The Viking Press, 1956.

Treen, Esmeralda and Alfred Treen. *The New Dalmatian: Coach Dog, Firehouse Dog*. New York: Howell Book House, 1992.

You can read articles about dalmatians in the magazines *AKC Gazette, Dalmatian Quarterly, Dog Fancy, Dog World,* and *Firehouse Quarterly.*

Useful Addresses

American Kennel Club
5580 Centerview Drive
Raleigh, NC 27606

Canadian Kennel Club
100-89 Skyway Avenue
Etobicoke, ON M9W 6R4
Canada

Dalmatian Club of America
1303 James Street
Rosenberg, TX 77471

Internet Sites

Welcome to the AKC
http://www.akc.org

Dalmatian Club of America
http://www.cet.com/~bholland/dca/

Welcome to k9web
http://www.k9Web.com

Index

anal sacs, 37

bath, 37
breeder, 39
brushing, 37

carriage, 8, 16, 19
coach dog, 11, 18

Dalmatia, 5, 13
Dalmatin, Jurij, 5, 15
diet, 36-37
Disney, Walt, 7

exercise, 27, 35

fire departments, 5, 19, 23,
   29-30
food, 36, 37

grooming, 37, 38
guide dog, 5
Gypsies, 15, 16

harrier, 16
horses, 8, 11, 13, 15, 16, 18,
   19, 21, 23, 33
hunting, 13, 17

mascot, 5

origin, 5

register, 5,
rescue shelter, 39
road trial, 33

search and rescue, 5, 29-30
Smith, Dodie, 7
spots, 5, 7, 8, 13, 25

uric acid, 27, 36, 37
urinary system, 27
U.S. Army, 30

veterinarian, 27, 38
withers, 4, 23